THE GREENING
OF THE SNOW BEACH

THE GREENING OF
THE SNOW BEACH

Carol Rumens

BLOODAXE BOOKS

ISBN: 1 85224 062 8

First published 1988 by
Bloodaxe Books Ltd,
P.O. Box 1SN,
Newcastle upon Tyne NE99 1SN.

Bloodaxe Books Ltd acknowledges
the financial assistance of Northern Arts.

Typesetting by Bryan Williamson, Manchester.

Printed in Great Britain by
Bell & Bain Limited, Glasgow, Scotland.

With love to Georgi Valentinovich
and his son, Yura

Acknowledgements

Acknowledgements are due to the editors of the following publications in which some of these poems first appeared: *First and Always* (Faber, 1988), *Gown, Illuminations, Partisan Review, P.E.N. New Poetry II* (Quartet, 1988), *Poetry Review, Strawberry Fields*, the *Sunday Times*, the *Times Literary Supplement* and *Yeats Club Review/Celtic Dawn*.

The drawings in *The Greening of the Snow Beach* are all by Jamie Jamieson-Black, except for the Carol Rumens cartoon on page 41. The photographs are by Carol Rumens.

Contents

OUTSIDERS

Foreign Affairs by Phone

They used to make me cry –
Your hushy consonants
And the forms of the vocative
– *ti, tvoi, tvoyar* –
Intimate as fingertips,
You finally confessed,
The handset warming
In your attentive grip.
In fact, I never ceased
To hear a declarative
And reverberating sigh
Touching a small ear, tensed
And eager and not far away –
Even when I'd advanced
Sufficiently to divine
That the probable topic was pig-farming
Or the new Astrakhan gas pipeline.

Due Back

A Leningrad-born emigré visits the Russian library, ULU

The Senate House, an ark devoid of graces,
Is lofty enough, at least, to vaporise
A memory of your city's more precise
And elevated *ports de bras* and *glissées*.

The afternoon glows plushly like a breath-cloud
Hung by a skier on an empty run.
You trudge the edge of crisping emerald lawn:
The cold clings to your scarfless throat, a death-shroud.

You disappear. The hungry, clustered trees
Stare with a burning, stoical compassion
And wait. Even the sun goes down with caution.
A little light is saved for your release.

Your polar dialect thaws at minus one.
You creep between the stacks on sibilant parquet,
Quick-eyed, entranced, bearing the date-stamp marking
Time, your tongue pressed to your heart, on loan.

Stella

I chew the venison
Though I'm nearly vegetarian
And talk to the shy
Picturesque across the table,
Swollen-lipped, round-eyed,
Herself a kind of fawn.
She's nineteen, used to dance
Until she got too tall.
Her awesome innocence
Would be alarming
If I were her parent
And had paid for her education.
Not being responsible,
I find her charming –
Even when she tells me
She's writing poems. Perhaps
I should offer to read them –
But why risk the collapse
Of so much empathy?

Uptable, the tempo
Is Slav and passionate –
Sardonic emigré wit
Versus Natasha,
Our guest of honour.
She's sort of mass-produced
Like one of those jumbo
Lacquered dolls that spill
Diminuendo
Strings of predictables.
She bears good news:
She's an evangelist:
Who are these sneerers
Who know so much about *glasnost*?
Of course, they're Jews.
She pleats her napkin
Into a vigorous fan.
She'd like to see them charged
Under Article Seventy –
Thoroughly purged.

Russia was home to us,
Stella and I agree,
When we were there...
But now it's here at home
Do we feel quite the same?
Stella says she does.
She's got that dangerous glow
For all things Russian –
Even the Soviet Union.
Oh yes I know, I know...
I add more of the sauce
That's like thinned marmalade
To obscure the taste of blood
Baked in tender sinew.
(It's time I took a stand
On this, fish too,
And even potatoes
With their weepy, inscrutable
Chorniye glaza.)
We smile through the cross-hatched
Chiaroscuro
Of crystal newly flushed
With Château Whatsitsname.
Oh yes, you're right, of course,
Revise furiously,
But don't throw out the drafts.
Our mild English voices
Scarcely comprehended
By anyone but us
Sink with love and shame
Into the unsurrendered
Dialect of a craft.

Chorniye glaza: Black eyes (also the
title of a sentimental gypsy ballad).

Explanations and Cassette
(including the theme music of *Dr Zhivago*)

1

This is a revolutionary song
But they are singing it in the emigrés' cafés:
How good we are to cut the bourgeoisie's necks!
They are changing this words, of course.

2

At first, didn't you know,
During this revolution
They have some private enterprise
So a woman is selling bublyechki.
For this
Bublyechki
Give me roublyechki!

Bublyechki are like doughnuts
But more dense.

3

Why do you look like this for?
You think it is banal
For your European taste?
The picture, of course, is quite rubbish
But, I am afraid, for the tune
He took something from my soul.

Welcome to the Club

Soviet Film Season foyer: birch trees, slogans
And sickles drowning in the day-for-night
Illumination, nosed by glooming shoals
Of your fellow-islanders, across whose polite

Post-imperial blah you catch the skirling
Rushy current of your native prose.
Your eyes slide at once to a hopeful angle,
Although already wise enough to suppose

The foreigner will not proclaim himself
By his shopping bag or his sentimental ways.
Even his premature ageing will have slowed
To the local rate; he will not look victimised.

Having defined one voice, you discover more
And more, emerging from the undergrowth
Like mushrooms, their fine threads spooling back
To a Urals cart-track

Or a Moscow park, but equally at home.
And you think of all the other loosened tongues
Convening for their particular celluloid dawn
Ritual beside the grey, incurious Thames –

A silent frieze of semaphors unfurled
Across the blank sheet of the metropolis
To an audience of kids who've seen the world,
And know it speaks English.

You move away, silent and self-contained,
To float somewhere among the subtitles.
The highlighted bas-relief of vowels
Gleams on the guilty air like the Elgin marbles.

The birch tree has become an endangered species,
Scarred horizontally with wounded eyes
And dried-up lips that must reserve their judgement –
Even their lies.

You've ceased to understand, you've ceased to listen.
You're left with culture and a weightless smile.
Don't be afraid. At least you're the man with the tickets
Not the girl in the overall.

A West Country Twin-Town

In the new year of our new life together
    When, dreamy, diffident
As stuttering English snow, we stole each other
    From history's Janus-glare,
And then, to cure our failure of intent,
    Glanced at a map, drove west
Towards the refuge of that kindest city –
    Fathered by Rome, but a true Hellenist,
Whose naiad waters, glorying in their own
    Warm, emerald climate, try to wash the frown
From marble rectitude: in that new year

A birch tree sidled up to welcome us
    Plaintively, a skinny city peasant
    Sighing the forest wasn't what it was,
And we, lounging in bed at noon, could count
    Through snow-dim glass a row
Of colonnades or pan-pipes, not convinced,
But happily suspecting that the pleasant
    Angel of English fantasy had swished
    Her wing across our view:
So we were held until the room went dark,
And vision sank to a shady glow of flesh...
    But midnight, scathing as a Bolshevik
Of love's imperial privacies, burst in
    And flung us out to public life again.
By one o'clock the city was a mess,
    Silent and slumped after the ritual shrieks
To *auld lang syne*, and dangerously chilled:
Even her dreams were limestone, moist and cold.

In that new year that wasn't a new start,
    Simply its shadow which, when lost,
Might still seem solider than all the rest,
    We watched grey water shrug itself along
In ruffled furs, and the mosquito snow
    Hugged by a ring of lamplight as it danced.
So deeply cold the sleeping city grew
    Each night that I believed her comatose,
Deaf to her naiads, fatally entranced.

Even the Renault seemed about to die;
Curled like a mercury-ball, a frozen mouse,
It could not raise a spark, but coughed
   With wincing shoulders, frail, tubercular,
While, from your rag-bound thumb, a hot, red tear
   Was futile, like all human sacrifice.

I was prepared never to get away:
   Now that you'd told me where we might have been,
I'd come to think that it was where we were,
   And every street could float off into sea.
Your 'most-premeditated' city, scarved
   In tremulous rivers, numberless bloodstreams,
   And yet unable to escape its dreams,
Had locked us into one stern homesickness,
   So even when we freed ourselves, our roads
   Would always take us north, and Bath appear
In memory's closing window like the ghost
   Of Petersburg at the start of each new year.

The Difference

My first time abroad,
I was nineteen or so
And crossing the laid-back pastures
Of Normandy in a train,
My forehead bumping the window,
When distant cows appeared.
I knew at once they were different.
French, I whispered, *French*,
Wishing I could hear them
Moo the Norman way.
And my first time in Moscow,
Only the other month,
I was crossing Herzen Street
In a shower of piano-scales
When, before I could stop myself,
Russian pianos, I thought
Wildly, *played by Russians!*
And the world streamed out again
Into an opened vista.
Whatever it was, that difference,
Unfathomable, possessed me;
My forehead jumped on the glass,
As if I were still as abroad,
As foreign as nineteen.

THE GREENING
OF THE SNOW BEACH

*A little scrapbook
of my first visit to the USSR*

29 MARCH – 12 APRIL 1987

What to bring with you

First and foremost, of course, a valid passport and a Soviet visa, and return tickets.

Moscow: A Short Guide
(Progress Publishers, 1979)

*

He saw better than she probably did what she meant by anonymous. It was all nameless the way everybody in a family was nameless; names were for strangers. All the shops and stores and warehouses here were in the family.

'One thing it's not meant to be like,' he said, 'is the States. Do you mind about that?'

'And yet,' she said, 'I keep getting a whiff of when I was a little girl. I wonder why that was. Do you know what I mean?'

'Perhaps,' said Paul, 'Russia is really everybody's past. Not everybody's future, but everybody's past.'

ANTHONY BURGESS
Honey for the Bears (1963)

Sunday, 22 March

Kolya phones his father in Moscow and tells him I'd like to go and see him while I'm there. After a short conversation, he comes back, discouraged. Apparently, Ivan Ivanovich is not at all keen to be visited by a strange English woman, even if she is his son's *padruga* (close friend).

Ivan Ivanovich was born in 1907. Until his retirement he held the rank of Rear Admiral in the Russian Navy. His political views were formed by Stalin, a leader not noted for his fascination with things Western. How doubly painful for him to have lost his only son to the "enemy". In the first letters he wrote to Kolya after his defection he called him a traitor. I had hoped to be an ambassador of better feelings between them...

Stalin was in fact addicted to Hollywood movies: cowboy, gangster, musical, romantic – the lot. Not surprisingly, they nourished his xenophobia. He believed that life in the West was as enviably decadent as shown on his private silver screen.

One of his minor purges: the removal of English words naturalised into Russian. In football, *penalty* became *shtrafni udar*. Foxtrot became *buistri tanets* – fast dance, and Tango, *medlyenni tanets* – slow dance. I never agreed with Auden that 'the Ogre cannot master speech'. On the contrary, that is one of the first thing he masters.

'The greatest humanist the world ever knew'
Fadayev, Stalin's obituary, *Novy Mir* (April 1953).

I would have been 8 when he died. I remember hearing his name on the wireless and I thought at first he was a bird, a huge and important Starling. Later I saw the picture of him lying in state and he still looked like a bird, a big dead one with a jutting, powder-white beak.

Wednesday, 25 March

Kolya rings his father again. This time he's very amenable. She can telephone when she gets to Moscow and we'll arrange something, he says. Kolya thinks he must have reported the possibility of my visit to the Authorities – and presumably received a shrugged, casual permission – a younger generation's 'So what?'

Am frightened out of my wits. What shall I say to him? I come in peace, take me to your leader? No, that's overdoing it slightly. *Dobryi Dyen, Ivan Ivanovich, eta Karol.* Better start practising: *Dobryi Dyen, Ivan Ivanovich, eta Karol!*

On the visa-form I shall tick Pleasure.
I am not a prodigal daughter or son.
I have not paid an arm and a leg for a one-way ticket.
I shall not climb a mountain of flashbulbs and interviews, gasping
Under the weight of that cardboard suitcase, remorse.
I shall not plead that I was kidnapped by MI5
Nor that I was seduced by a beautiful secret agent.
I shall not speak peace to peaceniks
Nor refusal to refuseniks nor dollars to black marketeers.
I shall not declare my secret loves.
I will not fall publicly and kiss the earth
Nor the boot gleaming on top of it.
                    A tourist
Ticks pleasure but remembers to complain,
Rattles the abacus in the hard currency shop,
Glints brazenly from a hotel cupboard,
Experiences slight turbulence over mountains.
A tourist is a father of vapour banished
By the first wind, leaving the sky as before –
Like a lake that has closed its lips over a drowning

Had no problems with the visa. So no one at the Russian Embassy reads my books either...

Kolya's definition of Glasnost:
    Freedom to speak about everything that's permitted.

23

Saturday, 28 March

We spend the whole day in Oxford Street, present-buying. I model leather jackets for Kolya's daughter; he vaguely thinks we're a similar size. I've never worn leather before, but, yes, I'd kill a calf to please him, dye the skin blue to enchant his daughter...

> I'm getting heavier, becoming too real.
> I'm a three-page letter, a page-three starlet.
> I'm a grief. A saved whale. A false Tsar. A blue guitar.
> I'm the Sunday when the clocks go forward
> Or back. I'm a dawn chameleon with soft, glossy skin
> That creaks when I turn in the mirror. A Frankenstein's monster
> Stitched intricately with pockets, armholes, buttons
> And a bloodless silk lining, under which my heart
> Is working harder and harder every minute.
> I'm the West. Rich. Munificent. It's a major rôle.

Packing, I put the tee-shirt with Lenin's head on top, so that if the customs people open my suitcase they'll see at once that I'm ideologically OK.

Our final Saturday night toast: Kolya looks at me with serious eyes as he raises the glass:
> *Dai Bog, nye noclyednaya!*
> *Please God, not the last*
>
> ...And now I wish I wasn't going.

Sunday, 29 March

In the car to Gatwick I look out at England for what feels, even more than usual, like the last time. (Is it really 6000 times safer in a jet plane than down here on the M25? Don't I mean 60? Or 6½?) The sky seems very tall with its heaped tiers of cumulo-nimbus. The trees have that tense, dark look of early spring, as if they're being pumped up to bursting with secret life. The almonds have already brimmed over.

Our tour-leader counts heads relievedly: everyone has turned up, on time, papers in order. The group is small and consists mainly of Russian language students, some still at school. They're all much, much younger than me – yet I still have the old, idiotic sense of being the youngest. My daughters, equally uneasy on the grounds of class-consciousness, conduct miniature sociological surveys from the sidelines. Oh communism, come quick....

...It comes, a slightly shabby plane with unsmiling staff. Not unfriendly, just not the saccharine nanny-dolls of the Western airlines. No competition, no PR. When we're airborne they serve us little cups of apple juice. It all feels pleasantly humdrum. I have a definite sense that my life is less endangered than usual.

I had hoped, in my ignorance, that we'd fly straight to Leningrad, where we'll be spending our first week, but no such luck: we have to disembark in Moscow and suffer the long haul of customs and immigration. This is a pain anywhere, but here there are additional hazards. For example, all jewellery has to be declared. After scanning my declaration-form the woman officer points wearily at the ring I'm wearing. 'Very cheap, very cheap,' I insist, 'not gold.' She waves me through while I'm still working out how to say 'it cost 75p in Top Shop'. All the women officers are beefy and sad-looking and middle-aged, all the men, young and thin and mean.

It was no surprise that the baby-faced customs officer
Fell in love with my new rucksack. She pushed it gently
Onto its side. It quivered, pleading virginity.
Her fingers melted over the crisp, scarlet folds of nylon,
The goldplated (surely?) zips, the tiny Japanese padlocks.
It gave itself up to her gracefully, yielding woman to woman.
Did she find love? Yes, of a kind. She found
Among the slippers and sweaters, the tampons and tickets, a folder
Containing poems ('Vashe?' 'Moye!') and the sheet music of
Stenka Razin.

Monday morning, 3 a.m.

The waiting Lethean submarine fills slowly
With the stumbling, sleepy reluctance of encumbered souls
Still unable to die to their lost time-zone.
We groan against the damp windows. The hero-city
Cannot bear to look at us. We disgrace the dead.
We insult the living, stoically asleep
In the high-rises, snoring their way to the six o'clock siren.
Replacing her blue-tinted glasses, our guide observes
The loss of face. She moves her tired hips quickly
To the front of the bus, and with her soft, clean English
Wakes up the microphone and appeases the shades:
To our left, to our right, straight ahead, the shadowy, the lost –
Grainy and dark as a conté-crayon drawing by Seurat –
Secretive as our windows. Closed, like our eyelids.

I am disappointed. I did not want my first sight of the bronze horse-
man to be a dim shape fleeing past a coach window. I wish she had
waited till tomorrow.

And now begins a nightmare of dim corridors and lifts, aching arms and fractured Russian, and longed-for doors that offer no refuge, although the Hotel is called *Gavan* (haven). At the desk I point out my 2 daughters and ask for a 3-bedded room. I am given a key. Up we go to the 5th floor with all our baggage. The room turns out to have only two beds. I go back to the desk, another key is complacently proffered. Back on another, even more distant corridor, the key unlocks a door with two beds behind it. I return to the desk. The process is repeated twice more with much fractious parleying with various *dejurnayas* in between. One of them takes some keys herself and goes hopefully from room to room. The only three-bedder is still in the disorder left by departed guests: 'No good, dirty,' says the girl hastily and shuts the door, though by now I'd be glad enough to fall into those tousled sheets, I can think of nothing pleasanter.

At last, a solution is reached (one I suggested much earlier, with no effect): we are given two two-bedded rooms between us. Exhausted, I manage to fall asleep to the noise of the first morning trams. After what seems like five minutes I'm wakened up by some kind of super-*dejurnaya* in medical-looking white overalls and briskly ordered to move myself and my two daughters to another room. Yes, of course, it contains just two beds. How extremely unsurprising. But don't worry, a boy will bring a bed. The secret of this room must be that it is the only one in the whole hotel to which boys can bring beds. Actually, the bed is brought with commendable speed by a strangely cheerful youth. No bedclothes... but never mind. It's time for lunch, and then the city tour.

The Greater Neva: ships, ice, blue plashings on the steps
(The tyres of the intourist coaches calmly chewing the kerbs).
Cameras, beaver-hats, shubas, anoraks, boots, pushchairs
Out on the edge of the windowy water, admiring the trade-routes –
So blue and spotless. Used matchsticks and lemon peel spirals
Are the only travellers, hurrying to see where everything
Ends or begins, determined to ride the bucking,
Prancing, white-horned, foamy-lipped bulls of Europa.

St Petersburg – Russia's first attempt at *glasnost* (glasnost, glasnost, echo the waves as they softly slap the concrete).

A tall schoolboy asks me for chewing gum as I walk along the Gribodayev Canal. *Nyet*. What about a pen? I offer him a blue felt-tip: he snatches it and rushes off in the opposite direction as if he thinks I'll call a militiaman, or try to take it back.

At last, the Bronze Horseman
Like everything else in this city, Falconet's statue is rather graceful and modest in scale. I circle it with my amateurish camera, trying to find an original angle – finally take its delicately snow-flecked backside.

Yemelian Khailov's Chernobyl
When the statue was being cast the mould suddenly cracked; molten lead gushed out and the workshop caught fire. Falconet ran away, but the foundryman, Yemelian Khailov, stayed behind and struggled to close the crack with clay. The cast was saved but Khailov was badly burned.

The Hermitage: Forget my remarks about the modest scale of the local architecture. As I climb the stairs into the yawning heights of marble and gold I suddenly know why there was a revolution.

Monday/Tuesday

Someone rings me late at night and shouts a stream of Russian in which the key word seems to be *igolka*. He asks me my room number. I don't understand, I say, and put the receiver down, feeling darkly threatened. This is it. THEY – whoever THEY are – have caught up with me. A few minutes later my door is rapped. Boldly flinging on my bathrobe, I open it. A young, pale, mustachioed man stands there, pointing to his stomach. *'Igolka,'* he says. I realise that he is pointing to where there should be a button on his jacket. Inspiration strikes: he wants a needle and thread. I oblige and think no more about it, but the next day he returns the needle and gives me a big bar of chocolate. He and another worker – both electrical engineers from Siberia – are sharing the room next door. That night we get together with a third Siberian, Slava, and drink vodka with bits of dry bread and cheese they have hoarded from breakfast. They say they like Margaret Thatcher very much and are surprised when I say I don't. Fortunately, we are in perfect agreement over Vysotsky.

They are delighted that I know his songs. They are decent and courteous: no one makes a pass, though they are disappointed that Kelsey and Becky sleepily insist on going to bed. The next day Brosi tries to persuade me to go for a sauna with him. I refuse politely. Later, they present me with a huge, beautiful gift-book about Leningrad, in which they have written, and a spray of carnations. Brosi the young *nachalnik* and his friend, an older, melancholy-looking man, are going back to Zirgut; Slava is going on to his sister's in Moscow. He gives me his phone number and asks me to ring him. He says he'll be on holiday till May.

The chambermaid, a sweet, plump country girl – one of fifteen children – has spotted the blue leather coat in my wardrobe, and begs me to sell it to her. I say I can't, it's a gift. Have I got any Chanel perfume, then? No such luck. In the end I give her a lipstick (old but unused) and some new coloured tights. She thanks me profusely.

Wednesday/Thursday

This is the city of Kolya's youth. He was born here. He spent his childhood in the Far East but returned at 16 to study at the Naval Academy, as his father had done. He met his first wife there ('a very sex-appeal girl' with a penchant for Admirals, who later ran off with a Hungarian singer...)

As I walk along the great, elegant concave of the Headquarters of the General Staff, I imagine how time might follow the same curve, and how I might find I have begun to walk into the past.

Kolya's youth: it somehow stands both in and outside time, like the buildings themselves. It is a presence; I could nearly creep up on it

and touch it. But it would be like trying to touch the buildings and trees, upside down in the shivering water.

Let there be lemon vodka instead – bright, citric, neon extinguisher....

Kolya has marked on my street-map the places of personal interest he wants me to photograph: his parents' flat on Ulitsa Pechatnikov (Street of Printers), his aunt's flat on Lomonosov Street, etc. I click my camera at likely-looking doorways.

> I am a lens, a map, a mission
> Spied on by each parked car, by each spade stuck in a snowhill.
> Babies in ski-suits widen their eyes at me.
> I peer at name-plates, numbers, I retrace my steps.
> I blink into a courtyard, wink at a railing, fall over a tramline.
> A traffic cop in a cage decides it's a comic strip
> Rather than a crime. It's about a funny woman tourist
> Trying to catch a Day in the Life of the Ordinary Russian People,
> And stuff it into her yellow carrier bag
> To show them at home when she hands out the Duty Frees.

One landmark is easy – the Admiralty. Again this exquisitely human sense of proportion: pillars and dome and needle-spire, topped with Mandelstam's 'aerial boat', all perfectly balanced as to height and mass, and that coarsest metal, gold, transmuted into a peculiarly heart-catching fragility. But how Kolya hated to go 'under the spire'. His political education began in his loathing of military drill, and reached the point of no return when, at the age of twenty-one, he was suspended, stripped of all status, including membership of the Komsomol, and imprisoned for a year – for failing to salute a senior officer and getting into a subsequent minor punch-up. 'Soviet society is a cage, the military establishment is a cage inside a cage, and I was put in a cage inside the cage inside the cage.'

Some little cadets are out sweeping the snow. Becky lifts her camera to them. They twirl their hips and adopt balletic poses with the instinctive showmanship of the militarily trained.

Friday, 3 April

Seventy years ago today Lenin arrived at the Finland Station and proclaimed the Revolution from the top of an armoured car to the assembled workers. His idea of revolution was actually quite different from theirs – international, somewhat abstract. But the hour was right and so the words hardly mattered.

To cross the lake between Sweden and Finland, Lenin and his party left their train and took two-seater sledges. About half way across, some of the men jumped out and made a dash across the ice towards the shore, overjoyed at being back on Greater Russian soil: the border guards, also moved, began embracing them. I re-shoot the film, keep them running, deeper and deeper into Russia; the train freezes to the rails, a blizzard begins, silence falls. What happens then: democracy, whirling up from the ground like loose snow, or the Tsar, ice-glued to his throne and getting icier, bigger?

Lenin arrived, of course: here's the armoured car, parked outside the Museum. And he hated publicity, poor man.

Becky and Kelsey decided to take a tram to the beach instead of going to the museum. They arrive back at lunchtime full of excitement. Becky has fallen through the ice up to her neck. She describes gleefully how *babushkas* pointed and tutted at her as she dripped her way home. The fur in her boots is sopping wet and has turned green. I stand them on the radiator pipe in the *dejurnaya*'s little kitchen. I predict they will remain wet for the rest of the entire trip. I turn out to be right.

Sunday, 5 April

We take the night train from Leningrad to Moscow. It's very slow, very dirty. How could one train produce so much tea and so little running water? Becky and Kelsey join a party of young people in another carriage. I lie awake on the hard bunk, waiting for them to come back. Midnight passes: I should go and search for them. But then they appear, very sober and rather disgruntled. They have apparently spent the entire evening arguing the dialectic of whether or not Kelsey should swap her Walkman for Sasha's lacquered box. The argument goes on: 'It's a very expensive box.' 'But I NEED MY WALKMAN.' Then the hopeful box-seller taps at our door. 'Get lost, Sasha,' says the Voice of Britain in unison. Sasha gets lost.

My first thought about Moscow in the grey morning light is that, though I imagined it would be huge and windy, it's even huger and windier. I don't think I shall like it.

As soon as I arrive at the Central House of Tourists (in fact far from central and favoured more by trades union delegations than tourists) I hurry to the public phones. I have my home-made phrase-book,

my purseful of kopeks...but how does a Russian phone actually work? I plead with a passer-by who is far too helpful: she performs the operation in one, unnerving second, and I'm through. Oh God, what was I going to say? Good evening, Ivan Ivanovich, I mean Good Morning. It's Kolya's friend, Carol. 'Where are you?' shouts the Admiral. 'Moscow.' 'Moscow?' he shouts, incredulous. 'When can I come and see you, I've got a little present' (loads of bloody presents, actually). He barks a time and day. 'I shall be waiting,' he shouts, and slams down the receiver. I feel as if I have taken my first step on the moon. What about a drop of lemon vodka to celebrate?

March 16	snow begins to thaw
April 12	the ice breaks up in the Moskva River
May 2	Moscow has its first thunderstorm
May 24	the apples blossom
August 26	leaves begin to fall
September 14	the first night frosts
October 28	the first snow
November 23	snow cover becomes general

(from *Moscow: A Short Guide*)

So I'm here between the beginning of the thaw and the breaking up of the ice...

38

Sunday/Monday

Into the Lenin Hills, not as rustic as they sound and neither white nor green, but an indeterminate spring grey. Grey, too, the swooping slide of the artificial ski-jump, the stone of the new University. Not finding much to do, we somehow get swept into a packed, candle-lit church. It turns out that a funeral is in progress. The corpse is displayed in an open coffin, but I, with my poet's powers of observation, manage not to notice it. Becky tells me about it afterwards in dramatic detail; how she will be haunted for ever by the old woman's ugly, mustachioed face.

Later we try to go to the Novodevichny Convent, but it's closed. As much else in Moscow will turn out to be, including the Tretyakov art gallery and the heated open-air swimming pool at Kropotkinskaya. *Renovation, prophylaxis* are words that reverberate throughout our stay – like *beriozka*, and *mineral water*.

I and a student friend decide to go to a full church service. We pick an accessible church at random on the map. It turns out not only to be functioning, but flourishing. A faded old tramp outside begs for kopeks. The faithful seem to have no qualms about money-lending in the temple, and inside, financial transactions concerning the purchase of candles continue throughout the service. It is a very odd mixture of intense devotion and the sort of casual standing-around-and-chatting you'd get in a market square. There is no clear-cut sense of the service beginning and the crowd builds all the time, pressing us nearer and nearer the iconostasis. Somewhere behind it is the priest. There are plenty of young people, even some children, but, no doubt about it, the *babushkas* are the militiamen of the religious life. The priest emerges, the high, monotonous Byzantine chanting of the invisible choir intensifies. Some of the old women are crying. One tells me off loudly, I don't know what for, I've hardly moved. A bird's cross-shaped shadow passes over the high, still-sunlit cupola. Another hour passes and the service shows no sign of finishing. We sneak out and go and buy some cakes at a street kiosk which also, unaccountably, sells chunks of cooked, gristly-looking meat.

Catch the PM on TV (every room boasts an enormous set) hectoring a member of the Politburo in tones that imply: I don't believe a word you say, my man.

Tuesday, 7 April

Follow the Prime Ministerial trail to Zagorsk. It's very picturesque, of course. But I'm beginning to feel I've had enough of disorganised religion and bossy *babushkas*. (This time, one of them excels herself by hitting a boy from our group in the stomach.) Every church and chapel is packed like a herring-barrel, and worshippers far outnumber tourists. I wander round outside in the slush, feeling bad-tempered. My mood is not improved by the constant sight of Becky's bare legs and soaked feet, now ineffectually wrapped in polythene bags. It's true her boots are still wet, but she could have worn more sensible shoes...

I purchase a bright red-and-pink scarf in the local *Beriozka*. Shall I wrap it round my head and go and thump a tourist?

What I will remember best about Zagorsk will be the lavatories – dim, stone caverns without doors, the enthroned babushkas calmly exposed to snow-flurries and stares. And Becky's feet – soaked, freezing, pink.

A NOTE ON WEST-EAST UNDERSTANDING
The letter X (zh) which, not long ago, the BBC emblazoned on the cover of their book, Russian Life and Language, *is the symbol commonly used for Ladies Room. It is also associated with an obscene word meaning "bum".*

Next official trip: Red Square. Like everything else in Moscow it's too big. We join the lengthily coiling line to get into the Mausoleum. The militia are a constant grey, twitching presence. They stare minutely at every individual as if we are all potential counter revolutionaries, jerk their chins and their bayonets and snap out orders: no loitering, hands out of pockets, move on there. (You don't even get time to decipher the Cyrillic on the gravestones, as if foreigners weren't really supposed to know that Stalin and Brezhnev are buried here.) We file into the dim-lit mausoleum – oh God, more religion.

'Inside it, in a crystal sacophagus, lies the body of Vladimir Ilyich Lenin, the great revolutionary and founder of the Communist Party of the Soviet Union and of the Soviet State, who died on 21 January 1924... A large monolith above the main portal bears the laconic inscription LENIN, *incrusted in dark red porphyry ...Please note that it is not permitted to enter either the Lenin Mausoleum or the Kremlin carrying a briefcase, carrier bag, parcel or so on.'* (Moscow: A Short Guide)

Is the tiny, dapper, baby-skinned saint really Vladimir Ilyich? We think so: surely if they'd made him out of wax they'd have tried for greater realism?

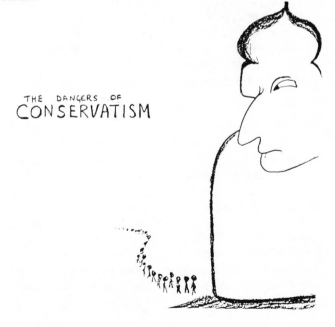

THE DANGERS OF
CONSERVATISM

Wednesday, 8 April

There's a coach trip into the centre of town for shopping. I take the opportunity of a lift to Kalininsky Prospekt. The driver is reluctant to stop there because of traffic regulations but, with the help of a pack of Marlboros from the Duty Free, I persuade him to apply his brakes for long enough to let me scramble off. Lumbering with my rucksack and suitcase towards what I hope is the Admiral's classy address (in the part of Moscow which, I've been told, is its Mayfair), I feel very calm, very determined. This, psychologically, must be the freedom that is the consciousness of necessity.

You sheltered by the tall apartment block
That lay its sallow shadow across the snow.
You were small in the buttoned-up greatcoat, an old campaigner
With a military style of patience –
But you stood to a different sort of attention
As you looked for me across the white backyards.
I came up by a side-path, uncertain
And more bewildered, now, by recognition.
I would have known you anywhere, each feature –
Though veiled and drawn a little closer to death –
The heart-shaped mouth set in chalky wrinkles,
The intent eyes, the lightly carried weight
Of one who has settled the question of himself
And has no reason to doubt it. You turn to me, smiling
With a sly satisfaction, as if you'd guessed
How often you have been kissed behind enemy lines.

The room we sit in used to be the bedroom where Kolya and his wife slept. There is a polished wooden floor, a big divan, a Turkish carpet hanging on one wall, a cabinet full of knick-knacks. Two porcelain tennis-players serve elegantly across the sideboard.

Lydia, Ivan Ivanovich's second wife, comes in from resting. She has a bad cough and is on a waiting-list to go into hospital. She is friendly, though her face has the severe look carved by illness. Her speed in making sense of my atrocious Russian is wonderful. We understood each other very well, she says when it's time to go. We begin with ceremoniousness: the teapot, a dish of jam, Lydia's meringues. The gifts are opened, photographs exchanged. Then somehow the table becomes covered with a vast party-like spread: tinned meats and fish and bottled salads and a huge Napoleon pie from the big fridge in the hall. Ivan wants to open the blue-label Smirnoff, but Lydia tells him he should save it for his birthday. So we drink our toasts in home-made rowanberry wine, which has been decanted into a variety of unsuitable bottles. Ivan gleefully points out the 'English' label on one of them: *Johnnie Walker Whisky.*

Ivan talks endlessly about Kolya's son and daughter, his only grand-children. I ask him where they're living now. Suddenly his eyes go shifty, and he starts to play the silly old man: dear me, d'you know, I've forgotten. Does he really think I'd be rash enough to turn up on their doorstep?

He is disappointed I haven't brought my children today. I hadn't realised Kolya had briefed him for the advent of the whole clan. I promise I'll bring them when I visit him again, on Saturday. He sees me back to the metro and kisses me goodbye; I feel so happy that when I get back to the hotel I bounce up and down on the bed like a two year old.

> The room was a blizzard of wrappings. Shapes emerged.
> Vodka: because "openness" doesn't apply
> To bottles containing gremlins, genies or genius;
> A camera – but can you get the film for it?
> A calculator – how long will the batteries last?
> Tracksuit, sweatsuit, a torch, vitamin pills –
> But if you run round the block in the snow your lungs can start
>   burning –
> A mug with a microchip glockenspiel in its base
> Pinging out 'Happy Birthday to you, Happy Birthday to you'
> But birthdays are often not happy, oh children, children...
> I could just see them, floating behind his broad shoulders
> A girl and a boy, wide-eyed, and the frightening ex-wife
> Looking frightened herself, gasping – is that why he left me! –
> About to fly into a rage, or fall in love again...

He asked me at one point: so when are you two going to register (i.e. get married)? I answered non-committally. And, in the sharp glance he gave me then, remembered how it had been to have a father.

Thursday/Friday

I have another visit to make: I can't put it off any longer. I have promised to call on the wife of an imprisoned dissident writer, with news of the English campaign for his release, and a small gift.

When I think of Ivan Ivanovich, I feel a momentary pang of guilt and even horror at my duplicity: I send it straight to the back of my mind.

The visit cannot be planned by telephone: I simply have to turn up. And I don't even know where the flat is: out somewhere in the suburbs, Sveta's street is on none of my maps, and no one I've thought OK to ask about it knows either. It's probably a bad decision, but one afternoon, sharing a taxi with some students who are also gift-bearing, I decide to ask the driver to take me on further, to S's street. He has to look it up in a kind of A-Z: it's a long way and will cost another seven roubles. I don't mind that. We set off: he is friendly enough and I am quite sure suspects nothing.

I find Sveta's block on a huge housing estate of high-rises. There is no one at home. I trudge around the district, discovering the bus routes and the nearest metro, so I won't have to take a taxi again. There is a vegetable kiosk: I've planned to bring Kolya back the taste of his native earth and so I join the queue of housewives and buy potatoes and cucumbers. The best way of getting talking to Russians is to join a queue. Someone always starts up a conversation – this time it's an old man, commenting on the eccentric purchases of the woman in front. She's buying huge quantities of raspberries – for home-made wine, no doubt. Then I go back and try Sveta's doorbell again: a dog barks but there's no reply.

I return the next evening and am lucky. She looks ill and tired but invites me in. She says there is hope of an amnesty for her husband. I give her the scarf and gloves and tell her that the campaign is gathering momentum. She nods sadly. I don't stay long: what is there to say?

The false, rosy charm of a standard lamp.
An unmade single bed. An abandoned desk.
Christ on the wall, trying to reach out and bless the photos
Of a shy young man, his unwritten books in his eyes.

I arrive back at the Centralnyi Dom in time to leave for the Circus.

МОСКОВСКИЙ ГОСУДАРСТВЕННЫЙ
Ц И Р К
НА ЛЕНИНСКИХ ГОРАХ

57 г.

ПРЕМЬЕРА

А. Братов, Ю. Архипцев

МОСКВА УЛЫБАЕТСЯ ВАМ
Эксцентрическая феерия в двух отделениях

песни И. Дорохова
Шаферана

Saturday, 11 April

I've been looking everywhere for a tin of *Chatka* crab for Kolya.
Finally I see one in the hotel's *Beriozka*. It costs 14 roubles. I take
it, and a tin of grapefruit juice for Lydia. The check-out girls
exchange glances as I pay my bill. I feel ashamed.

> Merchant-ambassadors of two provinces,
> They sit over the teapot, the bottles, the zakuski
> Telling the stories of their native lands.
> They compare the respective achievements of industry,
> Culture, research. They swap their wisest slogans
> Such as: *a man is guilty until proved innocent*
> Or: *a man is innocent until proved guilty.*
> Proudly they note the vast differences,
> The thread of shared ideals. Then, impulsively,
> One drains his glass and lowers his voice.
> Both provinces, he suggests, for all their attainments,
> Have suffered for many years from a secret plague –
> The Plague of things, or, to give it its medical name,
> The Plague of the Lack of Things. The other nods.
> Meditatively he pours the last drops. It can't be denied
> That in both provinces something in the air
> Seems to turn ideals into things, or the absence of things.
> They look at each other across the mountain of things
> They wish to exchange, being merchants. They ought not to smile
> Perhaps, in case smiles become things. They smile, anyway.

*'If ever a city expressed the character and peculiarities of its
inhabitants, that city is Moscow, 'The Heart of Russia' in which
the Russian 'Wide Nature'ı (shirokaya naturaı) is abundantly
obvious... What is here known as the "German" dress is predo-
minant but side by side with it we see the bearded muzhik in his
bast slippers, patched kaftan and grey armyak or sheepskin; the
Russian pope in his long brown robe, with his black hat and long
hair and beard; the merchant in his old-Russian fur cap, and his
wife adorned with strings of genuine pearls; Cirkassians, Tartars
and Bokhariots, all in their national dress; Greeks in red fezes;
Persians with high conical caps of black sheepskin; and other
types too numerous to mention. The various costumes of the lower
classes are best seen at the POPULAR FESTIVALS and in the
MARKETS.'* (Baedeker's Russia, 1914)

To Ivan's for lunch. We are slightly late, because I have been seduced by Dom Knigi on the way, especially by the cheap, pretty, pocket-sized books of poetry. I buy randomly, hoping to discover the new Soviet genius. I love the idea of pocket poetry books. But I suppose if any English publisher did it, it would come out twee – like those LT poetry posters which seem so desperately in need of a Maya-kovsky to design them. Which reminds me, I must actually look around at the architecture next time I take the metro. I am always so busy reading the signs I've never seen a single chandelier...But now it's already two o'clock: last purchases, please. Kelsey buys a lavish edition of *Anna Karenina*, in English. I can't resist an anti-vodka poster in shades of gloomy, cirrhosis-green. I shall hang it in the kitchen and take great pleasure in ignoring it.

Ivan meets us outside again. He is very pleased to see us. Lydia has gone into hospital, she has been waiting a long time and the summons finally came yesterday. He doesn't know how long it will be for. She has something wrong with her alveoli – he taps his chest sadly.

He is in the middle of cooking vegetables for our lunch: chips and onions in an iron pan. This is one of Kolya's favourites: he calls it 'Siberian potatoes'. It's delicious, and, of course, exactly right for the girls. He waits on their appetite with grandfatherly triumph. Then we drink some mournful toasts: to Lydia, absent from him, and to Kolya, absent from me. He only talks about Kolya's absence from his own life once: 'He never writes,' he says ruefully, looking at me as if he might be looking at the reason why. 'He doesn't know what to say' would be the honest reply – at least, it is the reason Kolya always gives and I know he means it. Instead I say: 'Please come and see us. We will meet you at the airport. We'd love you to come.' He shakes his head. 'I'm eighty years old, eighty years old!'

And politics? This is only mentioned in passing: Kolya was wrong when he said I'd be beaten about the head with propaganda. But I can't resist asking him what he thinks of Chairman Mikhail. His face lights up. 'Very much, very much. I like Margaret Thatcher very much too.' (This is called diplomacy, I think). 'Does she want war? We don't want war. Nobody wants it. We've had enough of war.' This isn't propaganda, either, but the truth, spoken by an old man who suddenly looks very tired.

Ivan's gifts: two bottles of rowanberry wine with seals improvised from baby-bottle teats, a copy of *Moscow: A Short Guide* (the Olympic Games edition), a packet of family photos, including one of Kolya, aged two, in a bib with his name embroidered on it, a bag of Lydia's meringues (she must bake thousands at a time) and two little brass goblets with vine-leaves entwining the rims. One for Kolya, one for me – so we can drink to each other, and to him…

'We don't want war. Nobody wants war, we've had enough of war'

Thrice-kissed under the chandeliers of Arbatskaya
I could sing like Okhudjava ('My Metro!'),
Dance a gopak, pray like a *babushka*
Blessing herself with veiny cross upon cross.
As we wave to each other through the gliding window
I know the exchange of gifts was nothing at all:
We vapourised them into infinity – love, remembrance,
Hope, forgiveness: *'Tell him I kiss him.'*
I shall be weightless, untaxable at the customs.
No one but you will ever find the three kisses,
Though they open my bags and the bags inside the bags.
Even the goblets will half evaporate…
We'll fill them tonight, and East and West will meet
With brimming lips, falling towards each other
As if nothing would ever part them again.

(Of course, Kolya said, women always like him, it's always the same, he's got a way with women. But his eyes were tender, conceding the unthinkable!)

REVOLUTIONARY MINIATURES

The Flood of Silence

*'What killed Pushkin was not d'Anthes' bullet; what killed
him was lack of air'* – Blok

*'What a Devil's Trick that I should be born with
a soul and talent in Russia'* – Pushkin

On London nights, Decemberish, icy,
When streets and sky and Thames are all
One shimmering cloth, gold-stippled, pricey;
When the wind hardens to a wall
On corners where theatres glitter,
And words are tossed away like litter
While golden eggs lay pizza-chains
And burger-bars and video-games,
I think of you in Tsarskoye Selo
Writing your ode to Liberty;
Bliss was it in that dawn to be
A dreamy, radical young fellow
Saved from Yakutsk, if not from court,
By exile of a milder sort.

I think how silence spreads its rivers
Over unstable, swampy banks;
Even the bronze-wrapped horseman shivers
As bridges float away in planks.
A wave shins up a lamp-post's rigging;
First doors, then balconies are swigging
The muddy water, then the chimes
Of plump St Isaac's; on it climbs...
Miraculously, we can hear you
Still, as if you were a bird –
Art with an olive-sprig – absurd
Image that surely fails to cheer you
As you gaze out of Leningrad,
Your mausoleum, huge and sad.

You built your ark, although the rising
Flood was almost at your throat –
A speedy, shapely, un-capsizing
Twentieth-century language-boat;
But still the future's uncreated
And writers with an elevated
Sense of buoyancy tend to drown
In deaths as airless as your own.
Brave actor, forced to play the gallant
When, in that proud, possessive place,
Adultery giggled in your face,
You died, having bemoaned your talent,
In shallow rivers of your blood –
Though you survive the greater flood.

The Duchess and the Assassin

The Grand Duchess Yelizaveta
Worried about the troops in Manchuria
While Sergei went on crushing the Revolution
In his silk-lined German carriage.

That afternoon of the palace sewing-bee
She was thinking about men's shirts,
Not of the bodies that might break in them,
Proving her perfect seams incontinent.

She watched the lazy bouncing
Of vulturish wrists, and knew it was for the best
That her mind should simply float...
She had drawn out the needle again –

The cotton had the strong pull of sunlight –
When the day went up like the Tsar's fleet at Tsushima.
She flung down the shirt and ran
Straight for the flushed smoke-cloud: silk and skin.

She picked up what she recognised
As the Governor-General, thinking: 'not my husband.'
Her apron sagged with the enormity...
The blood on her thighs screamed like birth-blood.

Clothes, after that, were water; even flesh
Showed her its inmost threading.
She sat, untouchable, by the opened curtains,
Burning her eyes on a lifetime of unpicking.

At last she came to the prison,
To the windowless cell, the stink of certainty.
She wanted to know why.
Even terrorists had their reasons.

He was nervous, and tried to sneer.
She felt her power. She wanted to lift her finger
To singe the skin of his cheek.
You don't understand. Forgiveness

Is the last thing I need, he said.
So you'll hang, Iván, she said.
His smile cleared: but the cause will outlive us both!
And she thought of the ripped halves

Of a shirt, stitched together
In stringy blood – two deaths,
Seamless, that Russia would wear
When it came to bury her.

Note: The Grand Duchess Yelizaveta, an exceptionally brave and intel-
ligent woman, was the sister-in-law of Tsar Nicholas II, and the wife
of the Governor General of Moscow, Sergei Alexandrovich, who was
universally disliked. He was assassinated at the Kremlin Gates by the
Socialist Revolutionary, Ivan Kalyayev, on 4 February 1917.

How the Tsar Tried to Restore Law and Order in Revolutionary Petrograd
A General Remembers

Martial Law Declared
By Order of the Council.
It was Golitsyn's last stand
In feathering pencil.

I rushed to the City Print-works,
Thrust a dumb cadet's
Nose at the signature:
He ran off fifty sheets.

Glue? I'd stopped a Gendarme.
Not for any honey-cakes!
There hadn't been a dribble
In Petrograd for weeks!

No glue, no soap, no strings
For fiddles. Them Red Guards
Must have been liberating
The knackers' yards.

After I'd rinsed his words
In a depthless glass, I hit
The streets, and met my Conscience
Again, looking like shit.

Paste, it muttered, *Flour*
And water. Flour? I said:
People are starving here.
My Conscience sank, half-dead.

Midnight. Sleet. Mud.
A smouldering police-station
Lit Sadovaya weirdly.
I was viewing my situation

As both historical
And unfortunate, when
The glinting tones of a railing –
Like a streetgirl's grin –

Leered at me from the gloom.
I was enticed, undone.
I spiked the Proclamations –
All fifty, one by one.

I strolled back to HQ
Thinking – What a devil
You are, Comrade Khabalov –
A secret rebel –

And how those paper wings
Would battle till they tore
Free and rode the wind!
So much for Martial Law –

Trampled and drowned in mud
And sweat and blood and sleet.
Like February, I'd washed
My dirty hands of it.

Conversation Piece
(loosely based on a sketch from
Fragments of my Diary by Maxim Gorki)

Petrograd, 1918.
They stroll in the Summer Garden
Discussing whether the masses
Deserve an education –

One believer, one doubter
From the poles of the social classes,
Bound by the fond condescension
That writer reserves for writer.

They sit down under a tree;
The masses are swarming about –
Soldiers and shop-girls and sailors
Where the Romanovs walked on glass.

Only the gardener's unchanged,
Impassively slaying the grass
In the haemophiliac rosebeds
While the little Tsarevich stares,

Turning paler, paler, paler.
Gorki gets out his pipe.
Blok crushes a lozenge of sunlight
With an apocalyptic boot

And denounces, as is his habit
The Intelligentsia's rôle.
Gorki the guttersnipe
Instantly loses his cool:

'The Intelligentsia drives
The engine of Progress. Your
Aristocratic contempt
Deserves a sock in the jaw!'

His cheeks shine tubercular red.
Blok looks at him strangely. The leaves
Of the ash tree scrape in his head
With a sound of puppet-strings, knives.

The smile of a passing laundress
Somehow changes the mood.
'Do you think there's a hope, old chap,
Of eternal life?' Blok mutters.

Cries Gorki: 'Of course it's eternal.
It's bloody miraculous
But everything's being recycled
Including the human race!'

'Listen. One late summer evening
Ten million evenings from this,
A shabby old pair of hacks,
Who should have something better to do,

Will be puffing out smoke and hot air
And explaining the Universe
As they sit on a bench and gaze
At a washer-girl's twinkling hips.'

Blok wrinkles his nose. 'You mean us?'
'Who else?' chortles Maxim, 'Who?'
Blok turns pale, he jumps up
In a fury of terror. 'You

Westernised heathen!' he shrieks.
'Thinking's the curse of the Slavs
And so I curse you and your granny!'
(Blok never does things by halves.)

Gorki sits calmly on,
Feeling sad for his fellow-writer.
The young moon rises and glows
White as a peeled onion

And the stars shine brighter and brighter.
'Revolution! Eternity!
Mankind!' whispers Gorki. The gardener
Goes home for a glass of tea.

Death of an Elder Brother

Stern-eyed Sasha, midnight reader,
Student of the worm,
Connoisseur of annelida,
How could he do harm?

Sasha spared his soily wrigglers,
Shunned the hook and knife.
But, said Sasha, Tsars are different
Lower forms of life.

There's a cause I'd gladly die for
Yes, and kill for too.
It's not natural, it's not moral
But what else to do?

Stern-eyed Sasha walks in leg-irons,
Clanking down the bight.
Ladoga laps, a workman taps
Out in the yard all night.

Sasha, Sasha, best Ulyanov,
Sobbed his brother, why
If you tried to save the people
Did you have to die?

In the young May dawn a broken
Life droops from a beam;
But the hempen rope binds stoutly
Dream to brother's dream.

Stern-eyed Sasha, midnight reader,
Student of the worm,
Connoisseur of annelida –
How could he do harm?

Note: Sasha (Alexander Ulyanov) was Lenin's elder brother. He was
hanged at the Oreshok Fortress, Lake Ladoga, on 5 May 1887,
for his part in the attempt to assassinate Tsar Alexander III.

ICE AND FIRE

A Moscow Wife, Waiting

Husbands wait sometimes, too:
But when I think of waiting,
I think only of you,

As if you were the true
Symbol of all waiting
And all who wait are you,

Larissa. And I see
The blackish lumps of snow
Surging to your dark porchway,

The flats in rows, the stairs
In hundreds, and I climb
Praying you'll be there,

Praying you won't be there.
I hear the clattered chains –
It's like a prison-door.

You peep an inch. I'm scared
I've scared you – and just scared.
But then – I've stepped inside.

You sit and listen, pale
Distracted. You look ill.
The message falters. No,

It isn't much. I can't
Say much. And there's a word
Which you repeat and which

Baffles me. That it means
The most important thing
For you is all I know.

'I'm sorry.' I bring out
My pocket dictionary.
The word is *amnesty*.

'You said 'I think there's hope.'
You didn't smile. I said
'I'm glad.' The words seemed small.

I took your hand, I went
Into the sleety cold.
And now I learn that hope

Was simply one more way
Of torturing you: they've sent
Your husband back to camp.

And yes, he's waiting, too;
But when I think of waiting
Somehow I think of you

As if you were the true
Symbol of all waiting,
And all who wait are you.

Note: Her husband was finally released at the end of May.

The Fire-Fighter's Widow
on her First Memorial Day Outing

We ride in the hired coach
North through April grey.
Spinneys of frail birch
Stagger up through the snow
Still rucked along the highway
As it rolls towards endless Moscow –
Nothing much else. We try
To lose ourselves in the view;
Pressed to our own faces,
We watch them travel with us,
Sickly, shut-out, like ghosts.
It was twelve months ago
That day our air was lit
Hugely and blown apart,
And still some people say –
Though they're not supposed to know –
Death hasn't gone away.

We're far, far North of green.
I'm glad to be so far,
Though they say the crops are clear
And plentiful this year,
I don't want to go near
Whatever our lives were then,
Between the rushing Pripyat
And the lake which never froze.
How warm and clean it was,
That water as it lapped
The broad towers of the plant –
Water that swept and cooled
The sun-packed rods, and kept
A little of their gold.
We fished (the fish were fat,
Sun-lazy), swam and dreamed.
Uranium was our friend
Until we forgot to fear it.
That was the night it turned.
The lake shrank in its heat;

Above the towers the air
Poured in savage plumes
As if the sun had been thrown
Earthwards. *His* grave is there.

He was a hero. We,
Therefore, are hero wives,
Trudging through burnt-out lives
And finding less and less,
However patiently
We stir the ash.
Pensioned, re-housed, redressed
By this Memorial Day
We wipe our eyes to say
None of it means a thing.
Surely our country's smashed
More heroes than it's worth?
I hate its giant hand
Which gathers men like clay
And moulds them into masses
To build red victories with.
They should have counted ten
Before they dashed away
And rose above the furnace,
Thinking they had to fling
Their lives down with the sand
In order to be men.

A Western scientist, one
Of those who built the Bomb,
In later life admitted
'I didn't think. I did
Experiments.' He's dust,
Now, in a Christian tomb,
And small as his regrets,
But if there was a God
Perhaps he'd be hauled back
Somehow across the years,
And made to ride with us.
He'd see what hope still is:
Our children, picnics, tears,
Our cheap new dresses, black:

He'd see the white graves
That now gleam into view,
Cleaner than any snow –
And leave the rest undone.

No other cemetery
Is quite as new as this –
The unplanted burial-ground
Of a spaced-out century.
There's no eternal flame
(As if they thought a glimpse
Of flame could drive us mad),
Only carnations, red
And dark as the burrowing
Roots of the meltdown.
Uniforms guide us through
Our public sorrowing.
Speeches drip their vowels
Through the muddy afternoon
Like ruined icicles.
We are praised, and shepherded.

Under us lie the dead
Heroes we used to know.
We watched them as they changed
Inside their unmarked skin –
Their useless, shivering courage,
Their shame as they vomited.
In a tangle of thick vines
All the good essences –
Saline, bone-marrow, blood –
Streamed down to rescue them
But sank in the rotting web
Of burning they'd become.
We touched them through our gloves,
Felt nothing. When they died
We were relieved. And then
Relief seemed out of date –
Like happiness, an echo
From life-times ago
When death was still a child,
Before it learned to breed.

We are the heroes' wives.
We are decaying too.
Some kneel beside the graves
Forgetting what they know –
That the world is a carelessness,
A chance in a universe.
Some weep. I'm not like these.
I simply walk away
And walk away, and then
The circle seems to close,
I'm back where I began,
Looking down in dismay
At the grass, the flowers, my shoes.

Leningrad Romance

1 *A Window Cut by Jealousy*

Not far from the estuary's grey window
They lit cigarettes and talked. Water kept meeting stone,
Lips kept sticking to paper, time kept burning.
The lilacs were burning down to the colour of stone.
She said, I was born here, I've lived here always.
Stone kept moving in water, time kept burning,
Smoke became palaces, palaces faded and faded.
My home's in Moscow, he said, my wife and children...
Perhaps they are just the white ash-fall of night,
Perhaps they are stone. Stone kept looking at shadows,
Shadows died in the white ash-fall of night.
Water kept playing with windows, time kept burning,
Fingers played with the burning dust of the lilacs,
The palaces faded and faded. I've lived here always,
She said, I've friends in Moscow. Thoughts became palaces,
Time went out, hands became estuaries,
The estuary was the colour of dying lilac.
They talked and lit cigarettes. Shadows flowed over the table.
They fingered them, but they didn't notice mine,
Not far from the estuary's grey window.

2 *Safe Period*

He will unlock the four-hooked gate of her bra,
Not noticing a kremlin built of lint,
With darkening scorch-marks where her arms press kisses.
She will pull back her arms, disturbing drifts
Of shallow, babyish hair, and let him drink,
Breathless, the heavy spirit smell, retreating
At length with a shy glance to grasp the chair-back,
And, slightly stooped, tug out the darker bandage.
Her cupped palm will glow as she carries it
Quickly to the sink, like something burning.
He sees the bright beard on each inner thigh,
Carnations curling, ribboning in the bowl.
Her hands make soapy love. The laundered rag
Weeps swift pink tears from the washing-string.
He's stiffened with a shocked assent. She breathes
Against him, damp as a glass. A glass of red vodka.

Finding the Sun

On Vasilievsky Island, brown and rumpled
With tramlines, stone in all its dreamed canals,
And plots still whispering through its plywood walls
I thought of the sun which Mandelstam had buried
In Petersburg, in the *velvet Soviet night*
And knew it lived, under the people's feet.

Wherever they trod, damp walkway planks or cobbles,
The crowds in their furry earflaps were trampling a thaw.
Rocks of soiled water loosened themselves
From the lips of drainpipes; soon, they'd dash for the river.
Spring's muddy pools would flower and the people know
That the time was ripe for exposing fragile earlobes.

In the meantime they went about hugged to themselves.
I thought of boats, their iron skirts swarming down
To the harbour-bed, lodging an iceberg's depth
Against a rusting anchor's mud-sunk sickle.
Dogged, they dreamed in queues, or butted the wind
Over bridges and through the arcades of Gostiny Dvor.

Darkness softly wrapped the great, flowing rush-hour
And still they were dawning and homing, those platoons,
Surging on their inscrutable manoeuvres.
They poured up from the burial pit of the metro
Like pyramid-builders, yoked by necessity.
Yet I saw how some had a secret happiness:

The militiaman in his heavy, mossy coat
Held a box of Napoleon pastry by its string
Daintily as a child's hand; a grey-faced woman
Lulled with her breath an armful of red carnations.
And in all the palaces rackety lifts crept up
Into night and the gleam of doors, bright-medalled with locks.

I sniffed a dialect, then, of *savoury pies,*
Pancakes, the evening samovar, soft sighs
And warm shawls and a hot stove to sleep on:
And the speeches lengthened, irremediable
In the lonely, jarring light of television –
But everyone wedged a chair in at the table.

Measured vistas, the seamless welding of Rome's
And Byzantium in gold as thin as skimmed milk,
Cannot contain the skyline of their hope.
It sinks and flickers, looking for depth, for stone,
And this is the point it rests at. Vasilievsky –
Where the poets will meet again and find the sun.

Quotations from Mandelstam, *Tristia* and Dostoyevsky, *Crime and Punishment.*

A Blockade Memorial

There were platoons of tents: not one was closed.
Inside, in each wound's dark, we knew there'd be
Pale puzzles like ourselves: a flawed yorick

At last conversant with his mess of props.
But when we dared to peep, the ossuary
Held simply straw, the light dormition of roses.

*

Since graves were everywhere, we couldn't see them.
The walkways bore them off to a last farewell –
A frayed red hand, waving up from the ground.

We trod on oak-leaves, stars – the splashed confetti
Of giant brides. The verb 'to die' is vast –
A city. But 'to die for the motherland'

Has no visible end, works in all tenses,
State-like, and makes them present: there are always
Live feet going over and over the dead.

*

An east wind, solid with processional ghosts
Carrying brands that first lit glowingly,
Then blanched, the faces of the crowd, swept through us

And drove us to the gates, the sheltering temples.
They frowned in pity, gathering the shades
Into their smaller, denser, human forms.

*

Here stood a country looking for itself.
First, it would find a baby's fist of bread –
The daily ration for 900 days –

And then, a diary. If the power-lines ceased
Their faintest song, and tyre-tracks, slithering,
Curved, for whatever reason, into silence,

If dry tongues ached against walls and shoe-leather –
How could a diary speak?
Somewhere there are girls who still know how.

*

She was called Tanya. Round her once had lived
Her family. True to girlhood courtesy,
She dipped her pen, listlessly, carefully;

As each one died, redeemed their gravelessness,
Making a loss-shape from the name and date
Until she had exhausted all her time

And reached her final name,
A child brought up to wait politely, take
The last turn in the complex grown-up game:

Everyone's died. Only Tanya's left.

*

Past the necropolis the earth lay snow-stilled
And empty, free to grieve in her own way –
Northerly, reticent. A concealed flood.

In moments we were tearless and absurd.
High-kicking, floundering through the half-whisked whites,
To storm the silver woods, our boot-tops foaming.

*

We found a pool. Dark water shivered thinly.
The adolescent birch trees seemed to step
Suddenly back, not liking to admit

How passionately they'd dwelt on their reflections.
Such slippages and slynesses and rumours!
We heard them, then: the ice-locks liquidly

Yielding, the wind more westerly
With each gust. But the lost weight of the starving
Still drifted from the camps: who'd cup its grains?

Distant, triumphal chords kept touching us
Like old soldiers vaguely fingering
Their medals, asking why there's so much dust

On swept and watered stones. And spring, too young
To hear them, stoops to the tents with a light breath:
She wakes the roses, snips the bandages.

Green Windows

Antarctica. Great plasterwork of gales.
The beach tumbled and whorled dull shades of white.
The surf a distant, quartzy heap of shale.

One step would crush the illusion. Underfoot
The relieved snow sank and fainted gushily.
More windows, glassy green, were breaking out

Each moment to the right and left of me –
For this was marsh, or would be, soon, a rippling
Of languid mosses tongued by the melt of sea.

I became strangely homesick for the coupling.
I longed to breathe its salts across the warm
Midsummer midnight's pale, circadian riddle.

Instead, I would be guided dully home
By the same trail that brought me here, and plod
My own deep, swampy prints – the paradigm

Of the tourist trapped in ever-widening odds
Against a revelation. In that slow
Defeat, I paused and stared. A rain of buds

I'd missed before shone round me: pussy willow –
In any sky or language, Proserpina,
Eyes starred with sleep, and mellowing as a rainbow.

And now her promise soothed a hemisphere,
Carefree of borders, seeping, roaming, greening:
A wash of flowers left at an English door.

A Memo About the Green Oranges

They sat like a disarmament proposal
On our table in the hotel dining-room,
Looking less and less negotiable.
Even the vegetarians flinched from them.

The Talks beside the lake weren't going well.
Neither was the turnover in these
Miniature ballistic atrocities –
Which now began to occur at every meal.

Oranges Are Oranges. Grass Is Green –
Like policemen's greatcoats. Never Trust A Red.
(It's better to be dead than dyed that shade.)
You Can't Tell A *Sosiska* By Its Skin...

But what about an orange? Feeling less
Hopeful than thirsty on Sadóvaya Street
One day, I bought a mossy half-a-kilo.

The Geneva Talks stand just as still, or stiller,
And this is simply a memo, a PS,
To say those green-skinned oranges are sweet.

TRANSLATIONS

'Noch, Ulitsa...'

Night: a street, a lamp, a chemist's;
Dreary, thought-erasing light.
Live another quarter-century –
Nothing's different. No way out.

Everything begins again,
Bearing the same old rubber-stamp:
Night: the freezing-cold canal,
The chemist's shop, the street, the lamp.

Aleksandr Blok

The Admiralty

In the Northern capital moulders a dusty poplar,
Its leaves entangling a clock's translucency,
And through the green darkness a frigate, an *akropol*,
Brother to water and sky, shines distantly.

An aerial boat with a mast like a touch-me-not flower,
A slide-rule for Peter's children, it declares
That Beauty's no whim from a demi-god's leisure-hour,
But a home-spun carpenter's predatory stares.

We honour the five reigning elements of creation:
Now a fifth, thanks to human freedom, has found its place –
An ark of such faultless design it asserts the negation
Of the tyranny of three-dimensional space.

Bad-tempered medusas jostle, exchanging their poison;
The abandoned ploughs of the anchors are tumbling to rust.
But look how the three dimensions burst from their prison
And the seas of the world lie open to us at last!

Osip Mandelstam

No, not the moon

No, not the moon, a clock; its homely face
Pouring down brightness. Am I in disgrace
For saying the stars are weak and watery?

Now Bátushkov – his was the real crime.
When people mildly asked him: 'What's the time?'
The crushing answer boomed: 'Infinity!'

Osip Mandelstam

'We'll die'

We'll die in crystalline Petropolis
Whose ruling deity is Proserpina.
We swallow deadly air with every breath
And every hour is like a year of death.
Goddess of oceans, terrible Athena,
Resign your helmet's stone magnificence.
We'll die in crystalline Petropolis
Which is not ruled by you, but Proserpina.

Osip Mandelstam

Kolya's Poem

I'm lucky. Russian-born, I think in Russian.
I eat my soup with bread instead of meat –
The Russian way. I dream and drink in Russian,
I even know the 'mother' oaths by heart,

Although I can't recall my actual mother.
I'm lucky. I've no friends. I feel no sadness
For anything on earth. I'm no one's lover.
I never fret about my circumstances.

If life is just, why should I start complaining?
What should I plead for if our needs are met?
Why should I sit behind the window, pining?
My day will come, the last and brightest yet.

Yes, it will come, that final, shining day
But, in the meantime, knuckle down, square up
And do the job. I'm lucky, certainly.
I wish my enemies this kind of luck.

*

Persephone in Armenia

The snow was a blue lake in Pushkin Square,
A twist of streams down Tsar Alexander Boulevard.
Buds split against the greenish
Luminous sky, rare as Cuban dates.
It was warm, it was burning, it was spring!
The girl moved swiftly with her blood-fall.
She tore off her coat,
Laced on her chilly sandals.
We didn't have time to stop her.
She was racing up the hill
Where snow-storms were massing again,
Her bare legs white with winter,
Plaits sparkling like iced wheat.